POCKET PROMISES
—*for*—
SPIRITUAL BATTLE

Encouragement in Daily Warfare

compiled by Anna Trimiew

Harold Shaw Publishers
Wheaton, Illinois

CONTENTS

INTRODUCTION

If you are a believer, committed to growing in your relationship with the Lord, then you need to have a clear picture of spiritual warfare. The Bible informs us that as we obey Christ, we become the enemy of evil, Satan, and the forces of hell.

Many of us are intimidated by warfare imagery and the idea of spiritual battle, and we certainly do not want our Christian walk to be one of conflict. Yet, if we are obedient Christians, we have no choice but to face hostile opposition.

However, the reassuring news is that the forces of evil have already been defeated. Satan and his troops cannot harm or destroy you, even though they will oppose you and try to influence you. In reality, the power of the Lord in your life alarms them, but they are committed to trouble-making and deception, and you are their target.

As you face conflict, may you find rest in the power and the victory of the risen Lord, and in the authority of his Word. Trust him to fight your battles. And may these words of faith and triumph encourage you as you live your life in obedience to God.

OUR REFUGE

At the heart of spiritual warfare is our reliance on God's presence even in the darkest moments of life. When we feel overwhelmed by circumstances, when we are losing our grip on life, when we see no end to the tunnel or feel that we are literally walking through the valley of death, we need to be able to turn to a God who sovereignly loves us.

A. Scott Moreau

He who dwells in the shelter of the Most High will rest in the shadow of the Almighty. I will say of the LORD, "He is my refuge and my fortress, my God, in whom I trust."
Psalm 91:1-2

The LORD is my stronghold, my fortress and my champion, my God, my rock where I find safety.
2 Samuel 22:2-3, NEB

He shall cover you with His feathers, And under His wings you shall take refuge; His faithfulness shall be your shield and buckler.
Psalm 91:4, NKJV

For the word of the Lord is right; and all His work is done in faithfulness.
Psalm 33:4, AMP

There is none like the God of Jeshurun who rides the heavens to your help, riding the clouds in his glory, who humbled the gods of old and subdued the ancient powers; who drove out the enemy before you and gave the word to destroy.

Deuteronomy 33:26-27, NEB

If you make the Most High your dwelling—even the LORD, who is my refuge—then no harm will befall you, no disaster will come near your tent.

Psalm 91:9-10

The LORD is a sure refuge for those who look to him in time of distress; he cares for all who seek his protection and brings them safely through the sweeping flood; he makes a final end of all who oppose him and pursues his enemies into darkness.

Nahum 1:7-8, NEB

And the Lord said, My presence shall
go with you, and I will give you rest.
Exodus 33:14, AMP

I want Jesus to walk with me,
I want Jesus to walk with me,
All along my pilgrim journey,
I want Jesus to walk with me.
Traditional Spiritual

My own sheep listen to my voice; I
know them and they follow me. I give
them eternal life and they shall never
perish; no one shall snatch them from
my care. My Father who has given
them to me is greater than all, and no
one can snatch them out of the Father's care.
John 10:27-29, NEB

You led your people, to make for
yourself a glorious name.
Isaiah 63:14, NRSV

Those who hope in Yahweh renew
their strength, they put out wings like
eagles. They run and do not grow
weary, walk and never tire.
Isaiah 40:31, JB

In my troubles, walk with me,
In my troubles, walk with me,
When my life becomes a burden,
Lord, I want Jesus to walk with me.
Traditional Spiritual

Keep alert, stand firm in your faith, be
courageous, be strong, Let all that you
do be done in love.
1 Corinthians 16:13-14, NRSV

"Because he loves me," says the LORD,
"I will rescue him; I will protect him,
for he acknowledges my name."
Psalm 91:14

Therefore God raised him to the heights and bestowed on him the name above all names, that at the name of Jesus every knee should bow—in heaven, on earth, and in the depths—and every tongue confess, "Jesus Christ is Lord", to the glory of God the Father.
Philippians 2:9-11, NEB

He will call upon me, and I will answer him; I will be with him in trouble, I will deliver him and honor him.
Psalm 91:15

When the righteous cry for help, the LORD hears, and rescues them from all their troubles. The LORD is near to the brokenhearted, and saves the crushed in spirit.
Psalm 34:17-18, NRSV

He is alive from the dead. He is victorious over all human ills. He has all the virtue and power of that victory in His own Person. He has been exalted and glorified in the presence of the Father, where He is active on our behalf.
Donald G. Mostrom

Be my Guide through all that is dark and doubtful. Be my Guard against all that threatens my spirit's welfare. Be my strength in time of testing. Gladden my heart with Thy peace; through Jesus Christ my Lord.
John Baillie

I have told you all this so that you will have peace of heart and mind. Here on earth you will have many trials and sorrows; but cheer up, for I have overcome the world.
John 16:33, TLB

FORCES OF EVIL

It is wrong to reject the existence of the powers of darkness, but it is equally wrong to believe in them in the wrong way.
Nigel Wright

And now war broke out in heaven, when Michael with his angels attacked the dragon. The dragon fought back with his angels, but they were defeated and driven out of heaven. The great dragon, the primeval serpent, known as the devil or Satan, who had deceived all the world, was hurled down to the earth and his angels were hurled down with him.
Revelation 12:7-9, JB

Do not turn to mediums or wizards; do not seek them out, to be defiled by them: I am the LORD your God.
Leviticus 19:31, NRSV

There are two equal and opposite errors into which our race can fall about the devils. One is to disbelieve in their existence. The other is to believe, and to feel an excessive and unhealthy interest in them. They themselves are

equally pleased by both errors, and hail a materialist or a magician with the same delight.
C. S. Lewis

Scripture acknowledges ... that objective spiritual beings have existed all the time, whether God, angels, Satan or evil spirits.
Donald G. Mostrom

A man or woman who is a medium or a wizard shall be put to death; they shall be stoned to death, their blood is upon them.
Leviticus 20:27, NRSV

On that day the LORD with his cruel and great and strong sword will punish Leviathan the fleeing serpent, Leviathan the twisting serpent, and he will kill the dragon that is in the sea.
Isaiah 27:1, NRSV

As he stepped out on land, a man of the city who had demons met him. For a long time he had worn no clothes, and he did not live in a house but in the tombs. When he saw Jesus, he fell down before him and shouted at the top of his voice, "What have you to do with me, Jesus, Son of the Most High God? I beg you, do not torment me"— for Jesus had commanded the unclean spirit to come out of the man. (For many times it had seized him; he was kept under guard and bound with chains and shackles, but he would break the bonds and be driven by the demon into the wilds.) Jesus then asked him, "What is your name?" He said, "Legion"; for many demons had entered him.

Luke 8:27-30, NRSV

And the teachers of the law who came down from Jerusalem said, "He is possessed by Beelzebub! By the prince of demons he is driving out demons." So Jesus called them and spoke to them in parables: "How can Satan drive out Satan? If a kingdom is divided against itself, that kingdom cannot stand."

Mark 3:22-24

I do not want you to be partners with demons.

1 Corinthians 10:20, NRSV

And I saw three evil spirits disguised as frogs leap from the mouth of the Dragon, the Creature, and his False Prophet. These miracle-working demons conferred with all the rulers of the world to gather them for battle against the Lord on that great coming Judgment Day of God Almighty.

Revelation 16:13-14, TLB

When you come into the land which
the LORD your God is giving you, do
not learn to imitate the abominable
customs of those other nations. Let no
one be found among you who makes
his son or daughter pass through fire,
no augur or soothsayer or diviner or
sorcerer, no one who casts spells or
traffics with ghosts and spirits, and no
necromancer. Those who do these
things are abominable to the LORD,
and it is because of these abominable
practices that the LORD your God is
driving them out before you. You shall
be whole-hearted in your service of
the LORD your God.

Deuteronomy 18:9-13, NEB

You have also established a new relationship with the powers of darkness.
Whatever you were before you became a Christian—straight, horo-
scope reader, witch, warlock or

Satanist—you are now the sworn foe
of the legions of hell.
John White

For we are not fighting against people
made of flesh and blood, but against
persons without bodies—the evil rulers of the unseen world, those mighty
satanic beings and great evil princes
of darkness who rule this world; and
against huge numbers of wicked spirits in the spirit world.
Ephesians 6:12, TLB

One thing which ought to animate us
to perpetual contest with the devil is,
that he is everywhere called both our
adversary and the adversary of God.
For, if the glory of God is dear to us,
as it ought to be, we ought to struggle
with all our might against him who
aims at the extinction of that glory.
John Calvin

RECOGNIZING THE ENEMY

There are many clear indications of Satan's motives and methods given us in the Bible, if only we would heed them. He is the arch-deceiver, adversary, accuser, the father of lies, and a "murderer from the beginning." His central purpose is to pull God from his throne in the minds of men and to take that throne himself.

R. Arthur Mathews

He who does what is sinful is of the devil, because the devil has been sinning from the beginning. The reason the Son of God appeared was to destroy the devil's work.
1 John 3:8

You were blameless in your ways from the day you were created till wickedness was found in you. . . . So I drove you in disgrace from the mount of God, and I expelled you, O guardian cherub, from among the fiery stones. Your heart became proud on account of your beauty, and you corrupted your wisdom because of your splendor. So I threw you to the earth; I made a spectacle of you.
Ezekiel 28:15-17

Now the serpent was more crafty than any of the wild animals the LORD God

had made. He said to the woman,
"Did God really say, . . . ?"
Genesis 3:1

Then he showed me the high priest
Joshua standing before the angel of
the LORD, and Satan standing at his
right hand to accuse him. And the
LORD said to Satan, "The LORD rebuke
you, O Satan! The LORD who has cho-
sen Jerusalem rebuke you!"
Zechariah 3:1-2, NRSV

How you have fallen from heaven, O
morning star, son of the dawn! You
have been cast down to the earth, you
who once laid low the nations! You
said in your heart, "I will ascend to
heaven; I will raise my throne above
the stars of God; I will sit enthroned
on the mount of assembly, on the ut-
most heights of the sacred mountain.
I will ascend above the tops of the

clouds; I will make myself like the Most High."
Isaiah 14:12-14

Be calm but vigilant, because your enemy the devil is prowling around like a roaring lion, looking for someone to eat.
1 Peter 5:8, JB

One day the heavenly beings came to present themselves before the LORD, and Satan also came among them. The LORD said to Satan, "Where have you come from?" Satan answered the LORD, "From going to and fro on the earth, and from walking up and down on it."
Job 1:6-7, NRSV

Satan himself masquerades as an angel of light.
2 Corinthians 11:14

The devil had already put it into the heart of Judas son of Simon Iscariot to betray him.
John 13:2, NRSV

I will not talk with you much more, for the prince (evil genius, ruler) of the world is coming. And he has no claim on Me—he has nothing in common with Me, there is nothing in Me that belongs to him, he has no power over Me.
John 14:30, AMP

Then Saul, who was also called Paul, filled with the Holy Spirit, looked straight at Elymas [the sorcerer] and said, "You are a child of the devil and an enemy of everything that is right! You are full of all kinds of deceit and trickery. Will you never stop perverting the right ways of the Lord?"
Acts 13:9-10

Some people act as though Satan is everywhere and knows everything. . . . This is wrong in light of biblical teachings. Satan is a limited creature, and we are called as Christians to engage in the battle against him.

A. Scott Moreau

Once you were under God's curse, doomed forever for your sins. You went along with the crowd and were just like all the others, full of sin, obeying Satan, the mighty prince of the power of the air, who is at work right now in the hearts of those who are against the Lord.

Ephesians 2:1-2, TLB

For we wanted to come to you—certainly I, Paul, did, again and again—but Satan stopped us.

1 Thessalonians 2:18

The hard pathway, where some of the
seed fell, represents the hard hearts of
some of those who hear God's mes-
sage; Satan comes at once to try to
make them forget it.
Mark 4:15, TLB

And ought not this woman, a daughter of Abraham whom Satan bound
for eighteen long years, be set free
from this bondage?
Luke 13:16, NRSV

There is in the world an enemy whom
we dare not ignore. We see him first in
the third chapter of Genesis and last
in the twentieth of Revelation, which
is to say that he was present at the
beginning of human history and will
be there at its earthly close.
A. W. Tozer

I saw Satan fall like lightning from heaven.
Luke 10:18

The God of peace will soon crush Satan beneath your feet.
Romans 16:20, NEB

Therefore rejoice, you heavens and you who dwell in them! But woe to the earth and the sea, because the devil has gone down to you! He is filled with fury, because he knows that his time is short.
Revelation 12:12

WARFARE WEAPONRY

On the battlefield the real enemy is fear and not the bayonet and the bullet.
Robert Jackson

Be strong in the Lord and in his mighty power. Put on the full armor of God so that you can take your stand against the devil's schemes.
Ephesians 6:10-11

We wield the weapons of righteousness in right hand and left.
2 Corinthians 6:7, NEB

For the weapons of our warfare are not physical (weapons of flesh and blood), but they are mighty before God for the overthrow and destruction of strongholds.
2 Corinthians 10:4, AMP

The night is far gone [and] the day is almost here. Let us then drop (fling away) the works and deeds of darkness and put on the [full] armor of light.
Romans 13:12, AMP

Stand firm then, with the belt of truth buckled around your waist, with the breastplate of righteousness in place, and with your feet fitted with the readiness that comes from the gospel of peace.

Ephesians 6:14-15

The weapons God has given us are not to be fired occasionally and then stored for future need. Rather, they involve daily, disciplined use lest we be overcome by the tricks and traps of the enemy.

A. Scott Moreau

King Jesus is our Captain, I shall not be moved;
King Jesus is our Captain, I shall not be moved;
Like a tree planted by the water, I shall not be moved.

Traditional Spiritual

Above all, taking the shield of faith with which you will be able to quench all the fiery darts of the wicked one. And take the helmet of salvation, and the sword of the Spirit, which is the word of God.
Ephesians 6:16-17, NKJV

For when Satan, strong and fully armed, guards his palace, it is safe— until someone stronger and better-armed attacks and overcomes him and strips him of his weapons and carries off his belongings. Anyone who is not for me is against me; if he isn't helping me, he is hurting my cause.
Luke 11:21-23, TLB

Discipline yourselves, keep alert.
1 Peter 5:8, NRSV

Unused weapons do not inflict casualties on the enemy nor win wars.
R. Arthur Mathews

Fighting sin and Satan, I shall not be moved;
Fighting sin and Satan, I shall not be moved;
Like a tree planted by the water, I shall not be moved.
Traditional Spiritual

And pray in the Spirit on all occasions with all kinds of prayers and requests. With this in mind, be alert and always keep on praying for all the saints.
Ephesians 6:18

So may all your enemies perish, O LORD! But may they who love you be like the sun when it rises in its strength.
Judges 5:31

BATTLE STRATEGY

If we are animated with proper zeal to maintain the kingdom of Christ, we must wage irreconcilable war with him who conspires its ruin . . . we ought to make no peace or truce with him who is continually laying schemes for its destruction.
John Calvin

The only way the devil can be rendered powerless today is as the truth and reality of the Savior's victory through his death on the cross is administered by the believer on earth operating in the name of the Lord Jesus Christ.
R. Arthur Mathews

Moses said to Joshua, "Choose some of our men and go out to fight the Amalekites. Tomorrow I will stand on top of the hill with the staff of God in my hands."
Exodus 17:9

So Joshua overcame the Amalekite army with the sword. . . . Moses built an altar and called it The LORD is my Banner. He said, "For hands were lifted up to the throne of the LORD."
Exodus 17:13, 15-16

And Joseph said to them, Fear not; for am I in the place of God? [Vengeance is His, not mine.] As for you, you thought evil against me; but God meant it for good.
Genesis 50:19-20, AMP

"But stretch out your hand now, and touch all that he has, and he will curse

you to your face." The LORD said to Satan, "Very well, all that he has is in your power; only do not stretch out your hand against him!" So Satan went out from the presence of the LORD.
Job 1:11-12, NRSV

Be submissive then to God. Stand up to the devil and he will turn and run.
James 4:7, NEB

Simon, Simon, Satan has asked to sift you as wheat. But I have prayed for you, Simon, that your faith may not fail.
Luke 22:31-32

The Bible makes it plain that we do not live in a dualistic universe, where there is a God of good and a god of evil—two equal and opposite kingdoms in a see-saw conflict. There is one God only, even though there is indeed a high-ranking creature who epitomizes rebellion and a spirit of independency, and who seeks with malice to usurp God's prerogatives and lord it over God's creation.

Donald G. Mostrom

If you are angry, don't sin by nursing your grudge. Don't let the sun go down with you still angry—get over it quickly; for when you are angry you give a mighty foothold to the devil.

Ephesians 4:26-27, TLB

If you forgive anyone, I also forgive him. And what I have forgiven—if there was anything to forgive—I have forgiven in the sight of Christ for your sake, in order that Satan might not outwit us. For we are not unaware of his schemes.

2 Corinthians 2:10-11

Now I'm on the battlefield for
 my Lord,
Yes, I'm on the battlefield for my Lord.
And I promise Him that I
Will serve Him till I die
'Cause I'm on the battlefield for
 my Lord.
Traditional Spiritual

Share in suffering like a good soldier
of Christ Jesus.
2 Timothy 2:3, NRSV

So fight gallantly, armed with faith
and a good conscience.
1 Timothy 1:18, NEB

Indeed, we live as human beings, but
we do not wage war according to human standards.
2 Corinthians 10:3, NRSV

Beloved, I urge you as aliens and exiles to abstain from the desires of the flesh that wage war against the soul.
1 Peter 2:11, NRSV

And having disarmed the powers and authorities, [Christ] made a public spectacle of them, triumphing over them by the cross.
Colossians 2:15

Uncovering the wiles of the devil can become so fascinating that we can begin to focus attention on the enemy rather than on God. This must be avoided at all costs. If we do it, we play into the enemy's hands.
C. Peter Wagner

And what more shall I say? I do not have time to tell about Gideon, Barak, Samson, Jephthah, David, Samuel and the prophets, who through faith

conquered kingdoms, administered
justice, and gained what was promised; who shut the mouths of lions,
quenched the fury of the flames, and
escaped the edge of the sword; whose
weakness was turned to strength; and
who became powerful in battle and
routed foreign armies.
Hebrews 11:32-34

You will not have to fight this battle.
Take up your positions; stand firm
and see the deliverance the LORD will
give you, O Judah and Jerusalem. Do
not be afraid; do not be discouraged.
Go out to face them tomorrow, and the
LORD will be with you.
2 Chronicles 20:17

For the Holy Spirit will teach you in
that very hour and moment what
[you] ought to say.
Luke 12:12, AMP

But if it is through the Spirit of God
that I cast devils out, then know that
the kingdom of God has overtaken
you.
Matthew 12:28, JB

God's gift was not a spirit of timidity,
but the Spirit of power and love and
self-control.
2 Timothy 1:7, JB

The LORD does not save by sword and
spear; for the battle is the LORD's.
1 Samuel 17:47, NRSV

God be praised, he gives us the victory through our Lord Jesus Christ.
1 Corinthians 15:57, NEB

Who is it that overcomes the world?
Only he who believes that Jesus is the
Son of God.
1 John 5:5

The night is nearly over; the day is almost here. So let us put aside the deeds of darkness and put on the armor of light. . . . Clothe yourselves with the Lord Jesus Christ, and do not think about how to gratify the desires of the sinful nature.
Romans 13:12, 14

Then this wicked one will appear, whom the Lord Jesus will burn up with the breath of his mouth and destroy by his presence when he returns.
2 Thessalonians 2:8, TLB

JESUS IN CONFLICT

Jesus came not only to deal with the problem of sin in the world, but also to deal with God's prime supernatural opponent—Satan himself.
Clinton Arnold

Then Jesus was led by the Spirit into the desert to be tempted by the devil. After fasting forty days and forty nights, he was hungry. The tempter came to him and said, "If you are the Son of God, tell these stones to become bread." Jesus answered, "It is written: 'Man does not live on bread alone, but on every word that comes from the mouth of God.' "

Matthew 4:1-4

"Moreover, if you set not your heart fixedly on Me, with a sincere wish to suffer all things for Me, you will not be able to bear the heat of this combat."

Thomas à Kempis

Then the devil took him to the holy city and had him stand on the highest point of the temple. "If you are the Son of God," he said, "throw

yourself down. . . . " Jesus answered
him, " . . . 'Do not put the Lord your
God to the test.' "
Matthew 4:5-7

Temptation is a factor in the psycho-
logical and spiritual growth process
everyone must go through if we are to
become mature individuals, capable
of living a full and meaningful life.
The function of temptation is always
to trigger a choice and provoke a defi-
nite stand or action.
Bob Mumford

Again, the devil took him to a very
high mountain and showed him all
the kingdoms of the world and their
splendor. "All this will I give you," he
said, "if you will bow down and worship me." Jesus said to him, "Away
from me, Satan! For it is written:

'Worship the Lord your God and
serve him only.' "
Matthew 4:8-10

Power in our lives comes by grace,
from the Holy Spirit, as we *walk* with
Him in yielded obedience.
Johanna Michaelsen

Then the devil left [Jesus], and behold,
angels came and ministered to Him.
Matthew 4:11, NKJV

Jesus breaks ev'ry fetter,
And he sets me free.
Anonymous

When Jesus saw that a crowd came
running together, he rebuked the unclean spirit, saying to it, "You spirit
that keeps this boy from speaking and
hearing, I command you, come out of
him, and never enter him again!" After

crying out and convulsing him terri-
bly, it came out. . . . When [Jesus] had
entered the house, his disciples asked
him privately, "Why could we not cast
it out?" He said to them, "This kind
can come out only through prayer."
Mark 9:25-26, 28, NRSV

For you are the children of your father
the devil and you love to do the evil
things he does. He was a murderer
from the beginning and a hater of
truth—there is not an iota of truth in
him. When he lies, it is perfectly nor-
mal; for he is the father of liars.
John 8:44, TLB

Jesus exclaimed in deep agitation of
spirit, "In truth, in very truth I tell you,
one of you is going to betray me. . . . It
is the man to whom I give this piece
of bread when I have dipped it in the
dish." Then, after dipping it in the

dish, he took it out and gave it to Judas
son of Simon Iscariot. As soon as Judas had received it Satan entered him.
Jesus said to him, "Do quickly what
you have to do."
John 13:21, 26-27, NEB

If . . . we can believe that God is in
complete control of our lives, that Satan can attack us only by His express
permission and only within the limits
that He sets, then we can hope that our
troubles are not for our harm but for
our good.
E. Calvin Beisner

Then Jesus told them, " . . . The time
of judgment for the world has come—
and the time when Satan, the prince of
this world, shall be cast out. And
when I am lifted up [on the cross], I
will draw everyone to me."
John 12:30-32, TLB

Since we, God's children, are human beings—made of flesh and blood—he became flesh and blood too by being born in human form; for only as a human being could he die and in dying break the power of the devil who had the power of death.

Hebrews 2:14, TLB

Jesus confronted evil firmly. But he did not ultimately overcome Satan by beating him up, but by loving others and submitting to God's plan of death on the cross.

A. Scott Moreau

THE CHURCH AT WAR

In God's topsy-turvy approach to power, he takes weak, scarred, scared, struggling, failing and ineffective people and accomplishes his mighty work with such miserably inadequate tools.

Richard Girard

You are Peter, a stone; and upon this rock I will build my church; and all the powers of hell shall not prevail against it.

Matthew 16:18, TLB

About midnight Paul and Silas were praying and singing hymns to God, and the other prisoners were listening to them. Suddenly there was such a violent earthquake that the foundations of the prison were shaken. At once all the prison doors flew open, and everybody's chains came loose. The jailer woke up, and when he saw the prison doors open, he drew his sword and was about to kill himself because he thought the prisoners had escaped. But Paul shouted, "Don't harm yourself! We are all here!" The jailer called for lights, rushed in and fell trembling before Paul and Silas. He then brought them out and asked,

"Sirs, what must I do to be saved?"
They replied, "Believe in the Lord
Jesus, and you will be saved—you
and your household."
Acts 16:25-31

He entered the synagogue and for
three months spoke out boldly, and
argued persuasively about the kingdom of God. When some stubbornly
refused to believe and spoke evil of
the Way before the congregation, he
left them, taking the disciples with
him, and argued daily in the lecture
hall of Tyrannus. This continued for
two years, so that all the residents of
Asia, both Jews and Greeks, heard the
word of the Lord.
Acts 19:8-10, NRSV

Christ is the Head of the church, Himself the Savior of [His] body.
Ephesians 5:23, AMP

You know what I was like when I
followed the Jewish religion—how I
went after the Christians mercilessly,
hunting them down and doing my
best to get rid of them all.
Galatians 1:13, TLB

He sends us out into the world as salt
and light even as He seasons the salt
and trims the wick. Healthy believers
recognize the growth process as a
natural one and welcome each other
as church members who are all (pas-
tor and board members, too) under
construction.
Joseph C. Aldrich

For what have I to do with judging
those outside? Is it not those who are
inside that you are to judge? God will
judge those outside. "Drive out the
wicked person from among you."
1 Corinthians 5:12-13, NRSV

But God has so arranged the body, giving the greater honor to the inferior member, that there may be no dissension within the body, but the members may have the same care for one another. If one member suffers, all suffer together with it; if one member is honored, all rejoice together with it.
1 Corinthians 12:24-26, NRSV

Now if we are children, then we are heirs—heirs of God and co-heirs with Christ, if indeed we share in his sufferings in order that we may also share in his glory.
Romans 8:17

We who are strong ought to put up with the failings of the weak, and not to please ourselves.
Romans 15:1, NRSV

I urge you, brothers and sisters, to keep an eye on those who cause dissensions and offenses, in opposition to the teaching that you have learned; avoid them. For such people do not serve our Lord Christ.
Romans 16:17-18, NRSV

Are you people in Galatia mad? Has someone put a spell on you, in spite of the plain explanation you have had of the crucifixion of Jesus Christ? . . . Are you foolish enough to end in outward observances what you began in the Spirit?
Galatians 3:1, 3, JB

Formerly, when you did not acknowledge God, you were the slaves of beings which in their nature are no gods. But now that you do acknowledge God—or rather, now that he has acknowledged you—how can you turn

back to the mean and beggarly spirits
of the elements?
Galatians 4:8-9, NEB

For you were called to freedom, brothers and sisters; only do not use your
freedom as an opportunity for self-in-
dulgence, but through love become
slaves to one another. For the whole
law is summed up in a single com-
mandment, "You shall love your
neighbor as yourself." If, however,
you bite and devour one another, take
care that you are not consumed by one
another.
Galatians 5:13-15, NRSV

The Church is a fellowship of the gospel, a society of the redeemed. No
more vivid picture of this is given us
than the "Church" of the Old Testa-
ment—Israel. Time and again the
Lord reminds them that the whole

basis of their unity as a nation is their deliverance from Egypt . . . and their inheritance of the Promised Land. The unity of the Church, too, lies in our redemption from the "Egypt" of sin and our common inheritance of eternal life.

David Winter

The LORD said, "I have indeed seen the misery of my people in Egypt. I have heard them crying out . . . and I am concerned about their suffering. So I have come down to rescue them from the hand of the Egyptians and to bring them up out of that land into a good and spacious land, a land flowing with milk and honey."

Exodus 3:7-8

The world would love you if you belonged to it; but you don't—for I

chose you to come out of the world,
and so it hates you.
John 15:19, TLB

Dear friends, do not be surprised at
the painful trial you are suffering, as
though something strange were hap-
pening to you. But rejoice that you
participate in the sufferings of Christ,
so that you may be overjoyed when
his glory is revealed.
1 Peter 4:12-13

There is one body and one Spirit, as
there is also one hope held out in
God's call to you; one Lord, one faith,
one baptism; one God and Father of
all, who is over all and through all and
in all.
Ephesians 4:4-6, NEB

The more we aspire to be perfect, the
more dependent we are on the grace

of God. We begin to need His help with every little thing and at every moment, because without it we can do nothing. The world, the flesh, and the devil wage a fierce and continuous war on our souls. If we weren't capable of humbly depending on God for assistance, our souls would be dragged down. Although this total dependence may sometimes go against our human nature, God takes great pleasure in it. That should bring us rest.

Brother Lawrence

For the Lamb standing in front of the throne will feed them and be their Shepherd and lead them to the springs of the Water of Life. And God will wipe their tears away.

Revelation 7:17, TLB

FIGHTING THE GOOD FIGHT

A Christian will find it cheaper to pardon than to resent. Forgiveness saves the expense of anger, the cost of hatred, the waste of spirits.
Hannah Moore

Put away from you all bitterness and wrath and anger and wrangling and slander, together with all malice, and be kind to one another, tenderhearted, forgiving one another, as God in Christ has forgiven you.

Ephesians 4:31-32, NRSV

Dear friends, never avenge yourselves. Leave that to God, for he has said that he will repay those who deserve it. [Don't take the law into your own hands.] Instead, feed your enemy if he is hungry. If he is thirsty give him something to drink and you will be "heaping coals of fire on his head." In other words, he will feel ashamed of himself for what he has done to you. Don't let evil get the upper hand but conquer evil by doing good.

Romans 12:19-21, TLB

If men would work redemptively in conflict situations in a world full of friction and violence, they must yield themselves in the spirit of Christ and His cross to become channels for God's saving love and power. Only thus do they truly follow in His trail. The cross, not the sword, is God's way of redemption.
Henry A. Fast

Then Peter came to Jesus and asked, "Lord, how many times shall I forgive my brother when he sins against me? Up to seven times?" Jesus answered, "I tell you, not seven times, but seventy-seven times."
Matthew 18:21-22

I appeal to you therefore, brothers and sisters, by the mercies of God, to present your bodies as a living sacrifice, holy and acceptable to God, which is your spiritual worship. Do not be conformed to this world, but be transformed by the renewing of your minds, so that you may discern what is the will of God—what is good and acceptable and perfect.

Romans 12:1-2, NRSV

Bold love is courageously setting aside our personal agenda to move humbly into the world of others with their well-being in view, willing to risk further pain in our souls, in order to be an aroma of life to some and an aroma of death to others.

Dan Allender and Tremper Longman III

Let love be genuine; hate what is evil, hold fast to what is good; love one another with mutual affection; outdo one another in showing honor. Do not lag in zeal, be ardent in spirit, serve

the Lord. Rejoice in hope, be patient in suffering, persevere in prayer.
Romans 12:9-12, NRSV

It is by love that the centrifugal force of sin is counteracted, for sin divides where love unites, and sin separates where love reconciles.
John R. W. Stott

But as for you . . . pursue righteousness, godliness, faith, love, endurance, gentleness. Fight the good fight of the faith.
1 Timothy 6:11-12, NRSV

I will say this: because these experiences I had were so tremendous, God was afraid I might be puffed up by them; so I was given a physical condition which has been a thorn in my flesh, a messenger from Satan to hurt and bother me, and prick my pride.

Three different times I begged God to
make me well again. Each time he
said, "No. But I am with you; that is
all you need. My power shows up best
in weak people."
2 Corinthians 12:7-9, TLB

"For I know the plans I have for you,"
declares the LORD, "plans to prosper
you and not to harm you, plans to give
you hope and a future. Then you will
call upon me and come and pray to
me, and I will listen to you. You will
seek me and find me when you seek
me with all your heart."
Jeremiah 29:11-13

MEASURING VICTORY

You don't have to outshout him or outmuscle him to be free of his influence. You just have to outtruth him. Believe, declare, and act upon the truth of God's Word, and you will thwart Satan's strategy.
Neil Anderson

I have heard of your faith in the Lord
Jesus and your love toward all the
saints, and for this reason I do not
cease to give thanks for you as I re-
member you in my prayers.
Ephesians 1:15-16, NRSV

God does not give us everything we
want, but he does fulfill all his prom-
ises, i.e., he remains the Lord of the
earth, he preserves his Church, con-
stantly renewing our faith and not
laying on us more than we can bear,
gladdening us with his nearness and
help, hearing our prayers, and lead-
ing us along the best and straightest
paths to himself. By his faithfulness in
doing this, God creates in us praise for
himself.
Dietrich Bonhoeffer

With God among us we shall fight like heroes, he will trample on our enemies.
Psalm 60:12, JB

And the devil, who deceived them, was thrown into the lake of burning sulfur, where the beast and the false prophet had been thrown. They will be tormented day and night for ever and ever.
Revelation 20:10

I pray that the God of our Lord Jesus Christ, the Father of glory, may give you a spirit of wisdom and revelation as you come to know him, so that, with the eyes of your heart enlightened, you may know what is the hope to which he has called you, what are the riches of his glorious inheritance among the saints, and what is the immeasurable greatness of his power for

us who believe, according to the working of his great power.
Ephesians 1:17-19, NRSV

For since he himself has now been through suffering and temptation, he knows what it is like when we suffer and are tempted, and he is wonderfully able to help us.
Hebrews 2:18, TLB

At times it is our reaction to suffering, rather than the suffering itself, that determines whether the experience is one of blessing or of blight. The same sun melts the butter and hardens the clay.
Paul E. Little

God put this power to work in Christ when he raised him from the dead and seated him at his right hand in the heavenly places, far above all rule and authority and power and dominion,

and above every name that is named, not only in this age but also in the age to come. And he has put all things under his feet and has made him the head over all things for the church, which is his body, the fullness of him who fills all in all.
Ephesians 1:20-23, NRSV

The power of spiritual weapons applied by insistent faith on conflict conditions cannot but thwart the enemy, bring victory to God's people, and fulfill his purposes.
R. Arthur Mathews

You were dead through the trespasses and sins in which you once lived, following the course of this world, following the ruler of the power of the air, the spirit that is now at work among those who are disobedient.
Ephesians 2:1-2, NRSV

I send you to open their eyes and turn them from darkness to light, from the dominion of Satan to God, so that, by trust in me, they may obtain forgiveness of sins, and a place with those whom God has made his own.
Acts 26:18, NEB

All of us once lived among them in the passions of our flesh, following the desires of flesh and senses, and we were by nature children of wrath, like everyone else.
Ephesians 2:3, NRSV

[The Father] has delivered and drawn us to Himself out of the control and the dominion of darkness and has transferred us into the kingdom of the Son of His love.
Colossians 1:13, AMP

But God, who is rich in mercy, out of the great love with which he loved us even when we were dead through our trespasses, made us alive together with Christ—by grace you have been saved—and raised us up with him and seated us with him in the heavenly places in Christ Jesus, so that in the ages to come he might show the immeasurable riches of his grace in kindness toward us in Christ Jesus.
Ephesians 2:4-7, NRSV

You need to persevere so that when you have done the will of God, you will receive what he has promised.
Hebrews 10:36

Comfort those who are frightened; take tender care of those who are weak; and be patient with everyone. See that no one pays back evil for evil, but always try to do good to each other and to everyone else. Always be joyful. Always keep on praying. No matter what happens, always be thankful, for this is God's will for you who belong to Christ Jesus.

1 Thessalonians 5:14-18, TLB

And the peace of God, which transcends all understanding, will guard your hearts and your minds in Christ Jesus.

Philippians 4:7

NOTES

NOTES

NOTES

NOTES

NOTES

NOTES

NOTES

NOTES

NOTES

NOTES

NOTES

NOTES

NOTES

NOTES

NOTES

NOTES